Writing Pron

24

W̶ ̶r̶i̶t̶i̶n̶g̶ Prompts
to Spark Ideas
for a Year

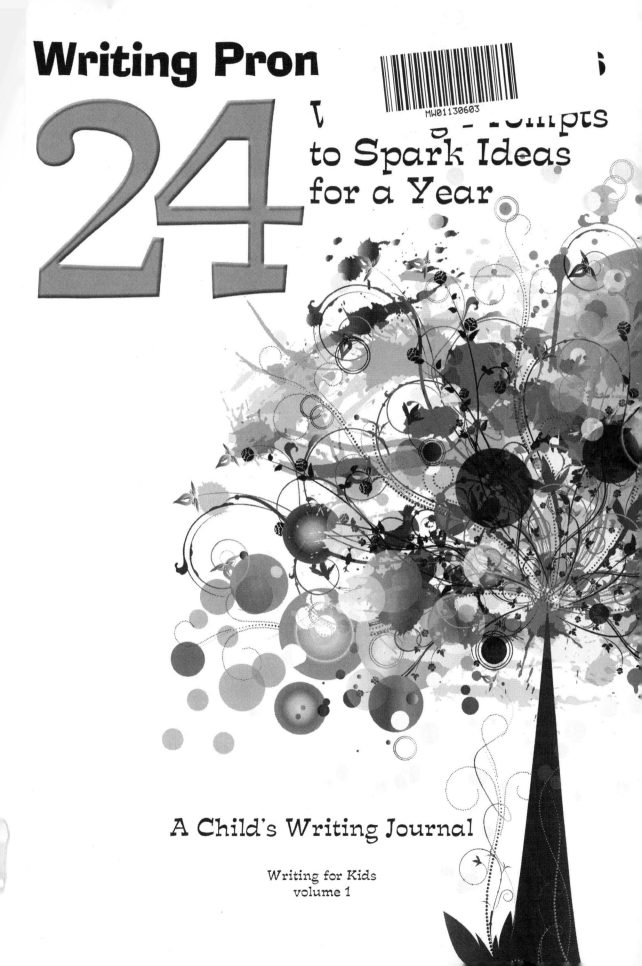

A Child's Writing Journal

Writing for Kids
volume 1

A note for parents:

I created this guided journal for all the kids out there who love to write. Inside, you'll find writing prompts, guided creation questions, doodle pages to spark storytelling visually, pages to write their stories on, and pages where your child can create their own book covers.

It's suitable for children betwen the ages of 7 and 12. After that, they get a little too mature for these kinds of prompts.

Give them colored pencils or markers and let them go crazy.

I'd love to read the stories and see the book covers! Share the covers on Twitter and tag me:

@WriteJoMichaels

To share the stories, take a photo and share on my Facebook page:

facebook.com/WriteJoMichaels

I hope your children enjoy using this journal, and I hope you hang on to it as a keepsake from their youth.

Writing Promps for Kids
24 Writing Prompts to Spark Ideas for a Year
A Child's Writing Journal
by Jo Michaels

©2015 Jo Michaels
First Printed Edition
Writing for Kids Volume I

ISBN-13: 978-1519410894
ISBN-10: 1519410891

Published in the United States of America

Cover design by Jo Michaels

Read me before you begin!

Hiya! If you're reading this, that means you have parents that love you and want to encourage your writing. That's amazing! You should tell them thank you for their support. :)

Here's how to use this book:

Each section has a start page where I give you some questions to help you come up with your big idea. Then, you go create a character and make decisions all your own. There's a lot to fill out, but it will be worth it!

After that, you get to create a book cover!

Finally, you get space to write and draw scenes!

Most of all, HAVE FUN!

Story 1

Here's your idea:

Think of a time you were scared.
What were you scared of?
How could you be braver?
What power would you like to have to help?

What is my character's name?

_____

Girl or Boy?

_____

How old?

_____

Is he/she human?

_____

If no, what is he/she?

_____

What is he or she going to try to do?

_____

_____

_____

Why? What started it?

_____

_____

_____

What are Mom and Dad's names?

_____

_____

Where do they live?

_____

_____

_____

What does my character look like?
Hair color:

_____

Eye color:

_____

Height:

_____

Weight:

_____

What kind of clothes does he/she like to wear?

_____

_____

What does his/her house look like?

_____

_____

Who is the bad guy/girl?

_____

Why is he/she bad?

_____

_____

How will he/she cause problems for my character?

_____

_____

Will there be any creatures in this book?

_____

If yes, what kind?

_____

_____

Where are they found?

_____

What do they eat?

_____

_____

Who are my character's friends?

_____

_____

_____

Why are they friends?

_____

_____

Are they human?

_____

If no, what kind of creatures are they?

_____
_____
_____

Where are they from?

_____
_____
_____

Does anyone have magical powers?

_____

What are they, and how are they used?

_____
_____
_____
_____
_____
_____
_____

My book title is:

_____
_____

Great! Now go to the next page and draw your cover!

Book Cover

Story 1

Story 1

Story 1

Story 1

DOODLE TIME!

Draw a scene!

Draw a scene!

DOODLE TIME!

Story 1

Story 1

_____
_____
_____
_____
_____
_____
_____
_____
_____
_____
_____
_____
_____
_____
_____
_____
_____
_____
_____
_____
_____
_____
_____
_____
_____
_____
_____
_____
_____
_____
_____
_____
_____
_____

Story 1

Story 2

Here's your idea:

Remember the last time your mom made you clean your room?
What if she was an evil ogre and you were under her spell?
How do you escape?

What is my character's name?

_____

Girl or Boy?

_____

How old?

_____

Is he/she human?

_____

If no, what is he/she?

_____

What is he or she going to try to do?

_____

_____

_____

Why? What started it?

_____

_____

_____

What are Mom and Dad's names?

_____

_____

Where do they live?

_____

_____

_____

What does my character look like?
Hair color:

_____

Eye color:

_____

Height:

_____

Weight:

_____

What kind of clothes does he/she like to wear?

_____

_____

What does his/her house look like?

_____

_____

Who is the bad guy/girl?

_____

Why is he/she bad?

_____

_____

How will he/she cause problems for my character?

_____

_____

Will there be any creatures in this book?

_____

If yes, what kind?

_____

_____

Where are they found?

_____

What do they eat?

_____

_____

Who are my character's friends?

_____

_____

_____

Why are they friends?

_____

_____

Are they human?

_____

If no, what kind of creatures are they?

_____

_____

_____

Where are they from?

_____

_____

_____

Does anyone have magical powers?

_____

What are they, and how are they used?

_____

_____

_____

_____

_____

_____

_____

My book title is:

_____

_____

Great! Now go to the next page and draw your cover!

Book Cover

Story 2

Story 2

Story 2

Story 2

Draw a scene!

DOODLE TIME!

Draw a scene!

DOODLE TIME!

Story 2

Story 2

Story 2

Story 3

Here's your idea:

Does your dad ever get upset?
What if he turned into a dragon?
Who made him that way?
How can it be fixed?

What is my character's name?

_____

Girl or Boy?

_____

How old?

_____

Is he/she human?

_____

If no, what is he/she?

_____

What is he or she going to try to do?

_____

_____

_____

Why? What started it?

_____

_____

_____

What are Mom and Dad's names?

_____

_____

Where do they live?

_____

_____

_____

What does my character look like?
Hair color:

_____

Eye color:

_____

Height:

_____

Weight:

_____

What kind of clothes does he/she like to wear?

_____

_____

What does his/her house look like?

_____

_____

Who is the bad guy/girl?

_____

Why is he/she bad?

_____

_____

How will he/she cause problems for my character?

_____

_____

Will there be any creatures in this book?

_____

If yes, what kind?

_____

_____

Where are they found?

_____

What do they eat?

_____

_____

Who are my character's friends?

_____

_____

_____

Why are they friends?

_____

_____

Are they human?

_____

If no, what kind of creatures are they?

_____

_____

_____

Where are they from?

_____

_____

_____

Does anyone have magical powers?

_____

What are they, and how are they used?

_____

_____

_____

_____

_____

_____

My book title is:

_____

_____

Great! Now go to the next page and draw your cover!

Book Cover

Story 3

Story 3

Story 3

Story 3

Draw a scene!

DOODLE TIME!

Draw a scene!

DOODLE TIME!

Story 3

Story 3

Story 3

Story 4

Here's your idea:

Do you have a big or little brother or sister?
What if they could fly or turn invisible?
What kind of trouble would they get into?
How crazy would your mom be?
If you don't have a sibling, does a friend?

.

What is my character's name?

_____

Girl or Boy?

_____

How old?

_____

Is he/she human?

_____

If no, what is he/she?

_____

What is he or she going to try to do?

_____

_____

_____

Why? What started it?

_____

_____

_____

What are Mom and Dad's names?

_____

_____

Where do they live?

_____

_____

_____

What does my character look like?
Hair color:

_____

Eye color:

_____

Height:

_____

Weight:

_____

What kind of clothes does he/she like to wear?

_____

_____

What does his/her house look like?

_____

_____

Who is the bad guy/girl?

_____

Why is he/she bad?

_____

_____

How will he/she cause problems for my character?

_____

_____

Will there be any creatures in this book?

_____

If yes, what kind?

_____

_____

Where are they found?

_____

What do they eat?

_____

_____

Who are my character's friends?

_____

_____

_____

Why are they friends?

_____

_____

Are they human?

_____

If no, what kind of creatures are they?

_____

_____

_____

Where are they from?

_____

_____

_____

Does anyone have magical powers?

_____

What are they, and how are they used?

_____

_____

_____

_____

_____

_____

My book title is:

_____

_____

Great! Now go to the next page and draw your cover!

Book Cover

Story 4

Story 4

Story 4

Story 4

Draw a scene!

Draw a scene!

DOODLE TIME!

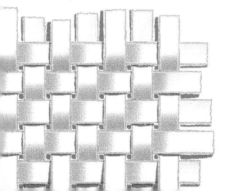

Story 4

Story 4

Story 4

Story 5

Here's your idea:

What if you had a box that could turn you into anything?
What would you choose to be?
Why?
What would you do?

What is my character's name?

_____

Girl or Boy?

_____

How old?

_____

Is he/she human?

_____

If no, what is he/she?

_____

What is he or she going to try to do?

_____

_____

_____

Why? What started it?

_____

_____

_____

What are Mom and Dad's names?

_____

_____

Where do they live?

_____

_____

_____

What does my character look like?
Hair color:

_____

Eye color:

_____

Height:

_____

Weight:

_____

What kind of clothes does he/she like to wear?

_____

_____

What does his/her house look like?

_____

_____

Who is the bad guy/girl?

_____

Why is he/she bad?

_____

_____

How will he/she cause problems for my character?

_____

_____

Will there be any creatures in this book?

_____

If yes, what kind?

_____

_____

Where are they found?

_____

What do they eat?

_____

_____

Who are my character's friends?

_____

_____

_____

Why are they friends?

_____

_____

Are they human?

_____

If no, what kind of creatures are they?

_____

_____

_____

Where are they from?

_____

_____

_____

Does anyone have magical powers?

_____

What are they, and how are they used?

_____

_____

_____

_____

_____

_____

My book title is:

_____

_____

Great! Now go to the next page and draw your cover!

Book Cover

Story 5

Story 5

Story 5

Story 5

Draw a scene!

DOODLE TIME!

Draw a scene!

DOODLE
TIME!

Story 5

Story 5

Story 5

Story 6

Here's your idea:

Aliens have landed on Earth.
What do they want?
How will you help?

What is my character's name?

_____

Girl or Boy?

_____

How old?

_____

Is he/she human?

_____

If no, what is he/she?

_____

What is he or she going to try to do?

_____

_____

_____

Why? What started it?

_____

_____

_____

What are Mom and Dad's names?

_____

_____

Where do they live?

_____

_____

_____

What does my character look like?
Hair color:

_____

Eye color:

_____

Height:

_____

Weight:

_____

What kind of clothes does he/she like to wear?

_____

_____

What does his/her house look like?

_____

_____

Who is the bad guy/girl?

_____

Why is he/she bad?

_____

_____

How will he/she cause problems for my character?

_____

_____

Will there be any creatures in this book?

_____

If yes, what kind?

_____

_____

Where are they found?

_____

What do they eat?

_____

_____

Who are my character's friends?

_____

_____

_____

Why are they friends?

_____

_____

Are they human?

_____

If no, what kind of creatures are they?

_____

_____

_____

Where are they from?

_____

_____

_____

Does anyone have magical powers?

_____

What are they, and how are they used?

_____

_____

_____

_____

_____

_____

My book title is:

_____

_____

Great! Now go to the next page and draw your cover!

Book Cover

Story 6

Story 6

Story 6

Story 6

Draw a scene!

DOODLE TIME!

Draw a scene!

DOODLE
TIME!

Story 6

Story 6

Story 6

Story 7

Here's your idea:

There's an elephant in school.
Why is it there?
What will it do?
How can you help?

What is my character's name?

_____

Girl or Boy?

_____

How old?

_____

Is he/she human?

_____

If no, what is he/she?

_____

What is he or she going to try to do?

_____

_____

_____

Why? What started it?

_____

_____

_____

What are Mom and Dad's names?

_____

_____

Where do they live?

_____

_____

_____

What does my character look like?
Hair color:

_____

Eye color:

_____

Height:

_____

Weight:

_____

What kind of clothes does he/she like to wear?

_____

_____

What does his/her house look like?

_____

_____

Who is the bad guy/girl?

_____

Why is he/she bad?

_____

_____

How will he/she cause problems for my character?

_____

_____

Will there be any creatures in this book?

_____

If yes, what kind?

_____

_____

Where are they found?

_____

What do they eat?

_____

_____

Who are my character's friends?

_____

_____

_____

Why are they friends?

_____

_____

Are they human?

_____

If no, what kind of creatures are they?

_____

_____

_____

Where are they from?

_____

_____

_____

Does anyone have magical powers?

_____

What are they, and how are they used?

_____

_____

_____

_____

_____

_____

My book title is:

_____

_____

Great! Now go to the next page and draw your cover!

Book Cover

Story 7

Story 7

Story 7

Story 7

Draw a scene!

DOODLE TIME!

Draw a scene!

DOODLE TIME!

Story 7

Story 7

Story 7

Story 8

Here's your idea:

You find out you're a queen or king from a distant
land.
Why didn't you know?
Why do you have to go home and rule?
What problems are there?

What is my character's name?

_____

Girl or Boy?

_____

How old?

_____

Is he/she human?

_____

If no, what is he/she?

_____

What is he or she going to try to do?

_____

_____

_____

Why? What started it?

_____

_____

_____

What are Mom and Dad's names?

_____

_____

Where do they live?

_____

_____

_____

What does my character look like?
Hair color:

_____

Eye color:

_____

Height:

_____

Weight:

_____

What kind of clothes does he/she like to wear?

_____

_____

What does his/her house look like?

_____

_____

Who is the bad guy/girl?

_____

Why is he/she bad?

_____

_____

How will he/she cause problems for my character?

_____

_____

Will there be any creatures in this book?

_____

If yes, what kind?

_____

_____

Where are they found?

_____

What do they eat?

_____

_____

Who are my character's friends?

_____

_____

_____

Why are they friends?

_____

_____

Are they human?

_____

If no, what kind of creatures are they?

_____

_____

_____

Where are they from?

_____

_____

_____

Does anyone have magical powers?

_____

What are they, and how are they used?

_____

_____

_____

_____

_____

_____

My book title is:

_____

_____

Great! Now go to the next page and draw your cover!

Book Cover

Story 8

Story 8

Story 8

Story 8

Draw a scene!

DOODLE TIME!

Draw a scene!

DOODLE
TIME!

Story 8

Story 8

Story 8

Story 9

Here's your idea:

Tiny creatures are in your kitchen cabinets.
What do they want?
What are they doing?
How do you make them go away?

What is my character's name?

_____

Girl or Boy?

_____

How old?

_____

Is he/she human?

_____

If no, what is he/she?

_____

What is he or she going to try to do?

_____

_____

_____

Why? What started it?

_____

_____

_____

What are Mom and Dad's names?

_____

_____

Where do they live?

_____

_____

_____

What does my character look like?
Hair color:

_____

Eye color:

_____

Height:

_____

Weight:

_____

What kind of clothes does he/she like to wear?

_____

_____

What does his/her house look like?

_____

_____

Who is the bad guy/girl?

_____

Why is he/she bad?

_____

_____

How will he/she cause problems for my character?

_____

_____

Will there be any creatures in this book?

_____

If yes, what kind?

_____

_____

Where are they found?

_____

What do they eat?

_____

_____

Who are my character's friends?

_____

_____

_____

Why are they friends?

_____

_____

Are they human?

_____

If no, what kind of creatures are they?

_____

_____

_____

Where are they from?

_____

_____

_____

Does anyone have magical powers?

_____

What are they, and how are they used?

_____

_____

_____

_____

_____

_____

_____

My book title is:

_____

_____

Great! Now go to the next page and draw your cover!

Book Cover

Story 9

Story 9

Story 9

Story 9

Draw a scene!

DOODLE
TIME!

Draw a scene!

DOODLE TIME!

Story 9

Story 9

Story 9

Story 10

Here's your idea:

Your grandmother is really a spy!
Who does she work for?
What's her secret weapon?
What's she doing?

What is my character's name?

_____

Girl or Boy?

_____

How old?

_____

Is he/she human?

_____

If no, what is he/she?

_____

What is he or she going to try to do?

_____

_____

_____

Why? What started it?

_____

_____

_____

What are Mom and Dad's names?

_____

_____

Where do they live?

_____

_____

_____

What does my character look like?
Hair color:

_____

Eye color:

_____

Height:

_____

Weight:

_____

What kind of clothes does he/she like to wear?

_____

_____

What does his/her house look like?

_____

_____

Who is the bad guy/girl?

_____

Why is he/she bad?

_____

_____

How will he/she cause problems for my character?

_____

_____

Will there be any creatures in this book?

_____

If yes, what kind?

_____

_____

Where are they found?

_____

What do they eat?

_____

_____

Who are my character's friends?

_____

_____

_____

Why are they friends?

_____

_____

Are they human?

_____

If no, what kind of creatures are they?

_____

_____

_____

Where are they from?

_____

_____

_____

Does anyone have magical powers?

_____

What are they, and how are they used?

_____

_____

_____

_____

_____

_____

My book title is:

_____

_____

Great! Now go to the next page and draw your cover!

Book Cover

Story 10

Story 10

Story 10

Story 10

Draw a scene!

DOODLE TIME!

Draw a scene!

DOODLE TIME!

Story 10

Story 10

Story 10

Story 11

Here's your idea:

Gnomes are in the garden.
What are they doing?
Can you talk to them?
Should you make them go away?

What is my character's name?

_____

Girl or Boy?

_____

How old?

_____

Is he/she human?

_____

If no, what is he/she?

_____

What is he or she going to try to do?

_____

_____

_____

Why? What started it?

_____

_____

_____

What are Mom and Dad's names?

_____

_____

Where do they live?

_____

_____

_____

What does my character look like?
Hair color:

_____

Eye color:

_____

Height:

_____

Weight:

_____

What kind of clothes does he/she like to wear?

_____

_____

What does his/her house look like?

_____

_____

Who is the bad guy/girl?

_____

Why is he/she bad?

_____

_____

How will he/she cause problems for my character?

_____

_____

Will there be any creatures in this book?

_____

If yes, what kind?

_____

_____

Where are they found?

_____

What do they eat?

_____

_____

Who are my character's friends?

_____

_____

_____

Why are they friends?

_____

_____

Are they human?

_____

If no, what kind of creatures are they?

_____

_____

_____

Where are they from?

_____

_____

_____

Does anyone have magical powers?

_____

What are they, and how are they used?

_____

_____

_____

_____

_____

_____

My book title is:

_____

_____

Great! Now go to the next page and draw your cover!

Book Cover

Story 11

Story 11

Story 11

Story 11

Draw a scene!

DOODLE TIME!

Draw a scene!

DOODLE TIME!

Story 11

Story 11

Story 11

Story 12

Here's your idea:

Your friend has a secret pet.
What is it?
How did they get it?
What will you do with it?

What is my character's name?

_____

Girl or Boy?

_____

How old?

_____

Is he/she human?

_____

If no, what is he/she?

_____

What is he or she going to try to do?

_____

_____

_____

Why? What started it?

_____

_____

_____

What are Mom and Dad's names?

_____

_____

Where do they live?

_____

_____

_____

What does my character look like?
Hair color:

_____

Eye color:

_____

Height:

_____

Weight:

_____

What kind of clothes does he/she like to wear?

_____

_____

What does his/her house look like?

_____

_____

Who is the bad guy/girl?

_____

Why is he/she bad?

_____

_____

How will he/she cause problems for my character?

_____

_____

Will there be any creatures in this book?

_____

If yes, what kind?

_____

_____

Where are they found?

_____

What do they eat?

_____

_____

Who are my character's friends?

_____

_____

_____

Why are they friends?

_____

_____

Are they human?

_____

If no, what kind of creatures are they?

_____

_____

_____

Where are they from?

_____

_____

_____

Does anyone have magical powers?

_____

What are they, and how are they used?

_____

_____

_____

_____

_____

_____

_____

My book title is:

_____

_____

Great! Now go to the next page and draw your cover!

Book Cover

Story 12

Story 12

Story 12

Story 12

Draw a scene!

DOODLE TIME!

Draw a scene!

DOODLE TIME!

Story 12

Story 12

Story 12

Story 13

Here's your idea:

You find out you're shrinking!
What problems are coming?
What can you do that's fun?
What will happen when you shrink all the way?

What is my character's name?

_____

Girl or Boy?

_____

How old?

_____

Is he/she human?

_____

If no, what is he/she?

_____

What is he or she going to try to do?

_____

_____

_____

Why? What started it?

_____

_____

_____

What are Mom and Dad's names?

_____

_____

Where do they live?

_____

_____

_____

What does my character look like?
Hair color:

_____

Eye color:

_____

Height:

_____

Weight:

_____

What kind of clothes does he/she like to wear?

_____

_____

What does his/her house look like?

_____

_____

Who is the bad guy/girl?

_____

Why is he/she bad?

_____

_____

How will he/she cause problems for my character?

_____

_____

Will there be any creatures in this book?

_____

If yes, what kind?

_____

_____

Where are they found?

_____

What do they eat?

_____

_____

Who are my character's friends?

_____

_____

_____

Why are they friends?

_____

_____

Are they human?

_____

If no, what kind of creatures are they?

_____

_____

_____

Where are they from?

_____

_____

_____

Does anyone have magical powers?

_____

What are they, and how are they used?

_____

_____

_____

_____

_____

_____

_____

My book title is:

_____

_____

Great! Now go to the next page and draw your cover!

Book Cover

Story 13

Story 13

Story 13

Story 13

Draw a scene!

DOODLE
TIME!

Draw a scene!

Story 13

Story 13

Story 13

Story 14

Here's your idea:

Your computer is talking to you.
What's it telling you?
Why?

What is my character's name?

_____

Girl or Boy?

_____

How old?

_____

Is he/she human?

_____

If no, what is he/she?

_____

What is he or she going to try to do?

_____

_____

_____

Why? What started it?

_____

_____

_____

What are Mom and Dad's names?

_____

_____

Where do they live?

_____

_____

_____

What does my character look like?
Hair color:

_____

Eye color:

_____

Height:

_____

Weight:

_____

What kind of clothes does he/she like to wear?

_____

_____

What does his/her house look like?

_____

_____

Who is the bad guy/girl?

_____

Why is he/she bad?

_____

_____

How will he/she cause problems for my character?

_____

_____

Will there be any creatures in this book?

_____

If yes, what kind?

_____

_____

Where are they found?

_____

What do they eat?

_____

_____

Who are my character's friends?

_____

_____

_____

Why are they friends?

_____

_____

Are they human?

_____

If no, what kind of creatures are they?

_____

_____

_____

Where are they from?

_____

_____

_____

Does anyone have magical powers?

_____

What are they, and how are they used?

_____

_____

_____

_____

_____

_____

My book title is:

_____

_____

Great! Now go to the next page and draw your cover!

Book Cover

Story 14

Story 14

Story 14

Story 14

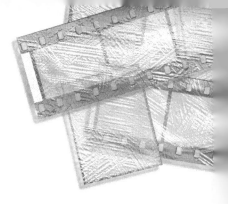

Draw a scene!

DOODLE TIME!

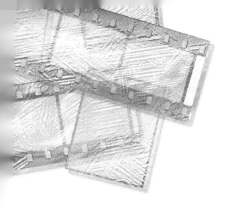

Draw a scene!

DOODLE TIME!

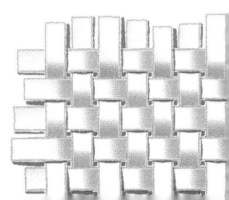

Story 14

Story 14

Story 14

Story 15

Here's your idea:

There's a cave near your house.
Bright lights can be seen coming from inside.
What are they?
How do you find out?

What is my character's name?

_____

Girl or Boy?

_____

How old?

_____

Is he/she human?

_____

If no, what is he/she?

_____

What is he or she going to try to do?

_____

_____

_____

Why? What started it?

_____

_____

_____

What are Mom and Dad's names?

_____

_____

Where do they live?

_____

_____

_____

What does my character look like?
Hair color:

_____

Eye color:

_____

Height:

_____

Weight:

_____

What kind of clothes does he/she like to wear?

_____

_____

What does his/her house look like?

_____

_____

Who is the bad guy/girl?

_____

Why is he/she bad?

_____

_____

How will he/she cause problems for my character?

_____

_____

Will there be any creatures in this book?

_____

If yes, what kind?

_____

_____

Where are they found?

_____

What do they eat?

_____

_____

Who are my character's friends?

_____

_____

Why are they friends?

_____

_____

Are they human?

_____

If no, what kind of creatures are they?

_____

_____

_____

Where are they from?

_____

_____

_____

Does anyone have magical powers?

_____

What are they, and how are they used?

_____

_____

_____

_____

_____

_____

_____

My book title is:

_____

_____

Great! Now go to the next page and draw your cover!

Book Cover

Story 15

Story 15

Story 15

Story 15

DOODLE TIME!

Draw a scene!

Draw a scene!

DOODLE TIME!

Story 15

Story 15

Story 15

Story 16

Here's your idea:

Slugs have been showered with mutant goo.
They're growing huge!
What happens?

What is my character's name?

_____

Girl or Boy?

_____

How old?

_____

Is he/she human?

_____

If no, what is he/she?

_____

What is he or she going to try to do?

_____

_____

_____

Why? What started it?

_____

_____

_____

What are Mom and Dad's names?

_____

_____

Where do they live?

_____

_____

_____

What does my character look like?
Hair color:

_____

Eye color:

_____

Height:

_____

Weight:

_____

What kind of clothes does he/she like to wear?

_____

_____

What does his/her house look like?

_____

_____

Who is the bad guy/girl?

_____

Why is he/she bad?

_____

_____

How will he/she cause problems for my character?

_____

_____

Will there be any creatures in this book?

_____

If yes, what kind?

_____

_____

Where are they found?

_____

What do they eat?

_____

_____

Who are my character's friends?

_____

_____

_____

Why are they friends?

_____

_____

Are they human?

_____

If no, what kind of creatures are they?

_____

_____

_____

Where are they from?

_____

_____

_____

Does anyone have magical powers?

_____

What are they, and how are they used?

_____

_____

_____

_____

_____

_____

My book title is:

_____

_____

Great! Now go to the next page and draw your cover!

Book Cover

Story 16

Story 16

Story 16

Story 16

Draw a scene!

DOODLE TIME!

Draw a scene!

DOODLE TIME!

Story 16

Story 16

Story 16

Story 17

Here's your idea:

Your friend just turned into a squirrel.
What caused it?
How can you fix it?

What is my character's name?

_____

Girl or Boy?

_____

How old?

_____

Is he/she human?

_____

If no, what is he/she?

_____

What is he or she going to try to do?

_____

_____

_____

Why? What started it?

_____

_____

_____

What are Mom and Dad's names?

_____

_____

Where do they live?

_____

_____

_____

What does my character look like?
Hair color:

_____

Eye color:

_____

Height:

_____

Weight:

_____

What kind of clothes does he/she like to wear?

_____

_____

What does his/her house look like?

_____

_____

Who is the bad guy/girl?

_____

Why is he/she bad?

_____

_____

How will he/she cause problems for my character?

_____

_____

Will there be any creatures in this book?

_____

If yes, what kind?

_____

_____

Where are they found?

_____

What do they eat?

_____

_____

Who are my character's friends?

_____

_____

_____

Why are they friends?

_____

_____

Are they human?

_____

If no, what kind of creatures are they?

_____

_____

_____

Where are they from?

_____

_____

_____

Does anyone have magical powers?

_____

What are they, and how are they used?

_____

_____

_____

_____

_____

_____

_____

My book title is:

_____

_____

Great! Now go to the next page and draw your cover!

.

Book Cover

Story 17

Story 17

Story 17

Story 17

Draw a scene!

DOODLE TIME!

Draw a scene!

DOODLE TIME!

Story 17

Story 17

Story 17

Story 18

Here's your idea:

Dragons!
You just found a dragon egg.
What will you do with it?
Why?

What is my character's name?

_____

Girl or Boy?

_____

How old?

_____

Is he/she human?

_____

If no, what is he/she?

_____

What is he or she going to try to do?

_____

_____

_____

Why? What started it?

_____

_____

_____

What are Mom and Dad's names?

_____

_____

Where do they live?

_____

_____

_____

What does my character look like?
Hair color:

_____

Eye color:

_____

Height:

_____

Weight:

_____

What kind of clothes does he/she like to wear?

_____

_____

What does his/her house look like?

_____

_____

Who is the bad guy/girl?

_____

Why is he/she bad?

_____

_____

How will he/she cause problems for my character?

_____

_____

Will there be any creatures in this book?

_____

If yes, what kind?

_____

_____

Where are they found?

_____

What do they eat?

_____

_____

Who are my character's friends?

_____

_____

_____

Why are they friends?

_____

_____

Are they human?

_____

If no, what kind of creatures are they?

_____

_____

_____

Where are they from?

_____

_____

_____

Does anyone have magical powers?

_____

What are they, and how are they used?

_____

_____

_____

_____

_____

_____

_____

My book title is:

_____

_____

Great! Now go to the next page and draw your cover!

Book Cover

Story 18

Story 18

Story 18

Story 18

Draw a scene!

DOODLE TIME!

Draw a scene!

DOODLE
TIME!

Story 18

Story 18

Story 18

Story 19

Here's your idea:

All people live in trees.
There is very little water left.
What happened to it all?
How do you fix it?

What is my character's name?

_____

Girl or Boy?

_____

How old?

_____

Is he/she human?

_____

If no, what is he/she?

_____

What is he or she going to try to do?

_____

_____

_____

Why? What started it?

_____

_____

_____

What are Mom and Dad's names?

_____

_____

Where do they live?

_____

_____

_____

What does my character look like?
Hair color:

_____

Eye color:

_____

Height:

_____

Weight:

_____

What kind of clothes does he/she like to wear?

_____

_____

What does his/her house look like?

_____

_____

Who is the bad guy/girl?

_____

Why is he/she bad?

_____

_____

How will he/she cause problems for my character?

_____

_____

Will there be any creatures in this book?

_____

If yes, what kind?

_____

_____

Where are they found?

_____

What do they eat?

_____

_____

Who are my character's friends?

_____

_____

_____

Why are they friends?

_____

_____

Are they human?

_____

If no, what kind of creatures are they?

_____

_____

_____

Where are they from?

_____

_____

_____

Does anyone have magical powers?

_____

What are they, and how are they used?

_____

_____

_____

_____

_____

_____

My book title is:

_____

_____

Great! Now go to the next page and draw your cover!

Book Cover

Story 19

Story 19

Story 19

Story 19

Draw a scene!

**DOODLE
TIME!**

Draw a scene!

DOODLE TIME!

Story 19

Story 19

Story 19

Story 20

Here's your idea:

There are no more computers or televisions.
How are things different?
What do you do to have fun?
What can you invent?

What is my character's name?

_____

Girl or Boy?

_____

How old?

_____

Is he/she human?

_____

If no, what is he/she?

_____

What is he or she going to try to do?

_____

_____

_____

Why? What started it?

_____

_____

_____

What are Mom and Dad's names?

_____

_____

Where do they live?

_____

_____

_____

What does my character look like?
Hair color:

_____

Eye color:

_____

Height:

_____

Weight:

_____

What kind of clothes does he/she like to wear?

_____

_____

What does his/her house look like?

_____

_____

Who is the bad guy/girl?

_____

Why is he/she bad?

_____

_____

How will he/she cause problems for my character?

_____

_____

Will there be any creatures in this book?

_____

If yes, what kind?

_____

_____

Where are they found?

_____

What do they eat?

_____

_____

Who are my character's friends?

_____

_____

_____

Why are they friends?

_____

_____

Are they human?

_____

If no, what kind of creatures are they?

_____

_____

_____

Where are they from?

_____

_____

_____

Does anyone have magical powers?

_____

What are they, and how are they used?

_____

_____

_____

_____

_____

_____

My book title is:

_____

_____

Great! Now go to the next page and draw your cover!

Book Cover

Story 20

Story 20

Story 20

Story 20

Draw a scene!

DOODLE TIME!

Draw a scene!

DOODLE
TIME!

Story 20

Story 20

Story 20

Story 21

Here's your idea:

Everything wants to eat you.
The toaster.
The trees.
Even your pet.
What happened to make them that way?
How can you fix it?

What is my character's name?

_____

Girl or Boy?

_____

How old?

_____

Is he/she human?

_____

If no, what is he/she?

_____

What is he or she going to try to do?

_____

_____

_____

Why? What started it?

_____

_____

_____

What are Mom and Dad's names?

_____

_____

Where do they live?

_____

_____

_____

What does my character look like?
Hair color:

_____

Eye color:

_____

Height:

_____

Weight:

_____

What kind of clothes does he/she like to wear?

_____

_____

What does his/her house look like?

_____

_____

Who is the bad guy/girl?

_____

Why is he/she bad?

_____

_____

How will he/she cause problems for my character?

_____

_____

Will there be any creatures in this book?

_____

If yes, what kind?

_____

_____

Where are they found?

_____

What do they eat?

_____

_____

Who are my character's friends?

_____

_____

_____

Why are they friends?

_____

_____

Are they human?

_____

If no, what kind of creatures are they?

_____

_____

_____

Where are they from?

_____

_____

_____

Does anyone have magical powers?

_____

What are they, and how are they used?

_____

_____

_____

_____

_____

_____

My book title is:

_____

_____

Great! Now go to the next page and draw your cover!

Book Cover

Story 21

Story 21

Story 21

Story 21

DOODLE TIME!

Draw a scene!

Draw a scene!

Story 21

Story 21

Story 21

Story 22

Here's your idea:

You have a special dog.
What can it do?
Why is that the coolest thing ever?
Someone tries to steal it.

What is my character's name?

_____

Girl or Boy?

_____

How old?

_____

Is he/she human?

_____

If no, what is he/she?

_____

What is he or she going to try to do?

_____

_____

_____

Why? What started it?

_____

_____

_____

What are Mom and Dad's names?

_____

_____

Where do they live?

_____

_____

_____

What does my character look like?
Hair color:

_____

Eye color:

_____

Height:

_____

Weight:

_____

What kind of clothes does he/she like to wear?

_____

_____

What does his/her house look like?

_____

_____

Who is the bad guy/girl?

_____

Why is he/she bad?

_____

_____

How will he/she cause problems for my character?

_____

_____

Will there be any creatures in this book?

_____

If yes, what kind?

_____

_____

Where are they found?

_____

What do they eat?

_____

_____

Who are my character's friends?

_____

_____

Why are they friends?

_____

_____

Are they human?

_____

If no, what kind of creatures are they?

_____

_____

_____

Where are they from?

_____

_____

_____

Does anyone have magical powers?

_____

What are they, and how are they used?

_____

_____

_____

_____

_____

_____

My book title is:

_____

_____

Great! Now go to the next page and draw your cover!

Book Cover

Story 22

Story 22

Story 22

Story 22

Draw a scene!

DOODLE TIME!

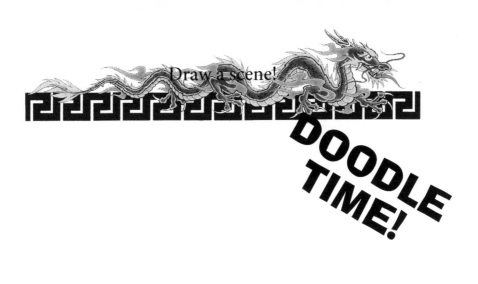

Draw a scene!

DOODLE
TIME!

Story 22

Story 22

Story 22

Story 23

Here's your idea:

You're on a quest to bring world peace.
What do you have to do?
What will happen if you fail?

What is my character's name?

_____

Girl or Boy?

_____

How old?

_____

Is he/she human?

_____

If no, what is he/she?

_____

What is he or she going to try to do?

_____

_____

_____

Why? What started it?

_____

_____

_____

What are Mom and Dad's names?

_____

_____

Where do they live?

_____

_____

_____

What does my character look like?
Hair color:

_____

Eye color:

_____

Height:

_____

Weight:

_____

What kind of clothes does he/she like to wear?

_____

_____

What does his/her house look like?

_____

_____

Who is the bad guy/girl?

_____

Why is he/she bad?

_____

_____

How will he/she cause problems for my character?

_____

_____

Will there be any creatures in this book?

_____

If yes, what kind?

_____

_____

Where are they found?

_____

What do they eat?

_____

_____

Who are my character's friends?

_____

_____

_____

Why are they friends?

_____

_____

Are they human?

_____

If no, what kind of creatures are they?

_____

_____

_____

Where are they from?

_____

_____

_____

Does anyone have magical powers?

_____

What are they, and how are they used?

_____

_____

_____

_____

_____

_____

My book title is:

_____

_____

Great! Now go to the next page and draw your cover!

Book Cover

Story 23

Story 23

Story 23

Story 23

Draw a scene!

DOODLE TIME!

Draw a scene!

DOODLE TIME!

Story 23

_____
_____
_____
_____
_____
_____
_____
_____
_____
_____
_____
_____
_____
_____
_____
_____
_____
_____
_____
_____
_____
_____
_____
_____
_____
_____
_____
_____
_____
_____
_____
_____

Story 23

Story 23

Story 24

Here's your idea:

You got a horse for your birthday!
Something is special about it.
What is it?
What will you do together?

What is my character's name?

_____

Girl or Boy?

_____

How old?

_____

Is he/she human?

_____

If no, what is he/she?

_____

What is he or she going to try to do?

_____

_____

_____

Why? What started it?

_____

_____

_____

What are Mom and Dad's names?

_____

_____

Where do they live?

_____

_____

_____

What does my character look like?
Hair color:

_____

Eye color:

_____

Height:

_____

Weight:

_____

What kind of clothes does he/she like to wear?

_____

_____

What does his/her house look like?

_____

_____

Who is the bad guy/girl?

_____

Why is he/she bad?

_____

_____

How will he/she cause problems for my character?

_____

_____

Will there be any creatures in this book?

_____

If yes, what kind?

_____

_____

Where are they found?

_____

What do they eat?

_____

_____

Who are my character's friends?

_____

_____

_____

Why are they friends?

_____

_____

Are they human?

_____

If no, what kind of creatures are they?

_____

_____

_____

Where are they from?

_____

_____

_____

Does anyone have magical powers?

_____

What are they, and how are they used?

_____

_____

_____

_____

_____

_____

My book title is:

_____

_____

Great! Now go to the next page and draw your cover!

Book Cover

Story 24

Story 24

Story 24

Story 24

Draw a scene!

DOODLE TIME!

Draw a scene!

DOODLE TIME!

Story 24

Story 24

Story 24

The End!

If you made it this far, you should pat yourself on the back!
You just wrote 24 stories! How amazing do you feel?

CONGRATULATIONS!

Be sure and visit my website for great books like:
The Frivolity Fairies: A Christmas Short Story (Free)
M
Fractured Glass
I, Zombie

Plus several free PDFs on the craft of writing.

You can find me here:
http://jomichaels.blogspot.com
www.WriteJoMichaels.com
@WriteJoMichaels
facebook.com/WriteJoMichaels

Thanks for purchasing this book. I hope you enjoyed writing in it!

43179659R00193

Made in the USA
San Bernardino, CA
12 July 2019